What Others Say about this Book

As a chiropractor, I believe that healing encompasses the mind, body, and spirit. *The Athena Treasury* makes my job easier by rejuvenating the mind and the spirit. A must, not only for my patients, but also for myself.

Misty Paul, D.C.
Owner, Central Valley Chiropractic

My goal for my life, and for women of all ages, is to become a Dynamite Old Lady! (Dynamite, from the Greek *dunamis* for power) My hope is that *The Athena Treasury* will empower and enable every woman who finds it by her bedside at our Inn.

Marlene Cartwright
Co-owner, High Country Inn Bed and Breakfast

A marvelous salute to women of all ages. Read it!

Cheewa James
Author, speaker and television personality

This collection is inspiring indeed. It can help women understand that the challenges we feel we face alone are shared with other women; that these challenges can be met; and that life can hold the joy and fulfillment we all seek if we make the decision to improve our lives and generate the courage to act on that decision.

Barbara Pletcher
Founder, National Association for Professional Saleswomen

Marty's new book is her second great tribute to her strong belief that *Attitude Works* (witness her publishing company's name). It certainly does! Thank you, Marty, for another inspiring book.

Wendy Slater
Owner, Aspen Typographix

Books by Marty Maskall

The Attitude Treasury:
101 Inspiring Quotations

The Athena Treasury:
101 Inspiring Quotations by Women

The Athena Treasury
101 Inspiring Quotations by Women

Edited by Marty Maskall

Foreword by Sally Edwards
Illustrated by Diane Carlson

Attitude Works Publishing Company
Fair Oaks, CA

The Athena Treasury
101 Inspiring Quotations by Women

Edited by Marty Maskall

Published by:
  Attitude Works Publishing Company
  Post Office Box 1765
  Fair Oaks, CA 95628
  916/967-2470

Cover design: Gaelyn and Bram Larrick,
                  Lightbourne Images
Illustrations: Diane Carlson
Printer: Griffin Printing

Publisher's Cataloging in Publication Data
The Athena Treasury: 101 Inspiring Quotations by
Women / edited by Marty Maskall; foreword by Sally
Edwards; illustrated by Diane Carlson --
p. cm.
Includes bibliographical references and indexes.

1. Quotations, English   2. Women—Quotations
I. Maskall, Marty, 1945-

PN6081   080A867   LC 93-70371
ISBN 0-9627670-3-4 $9.95 Softcover

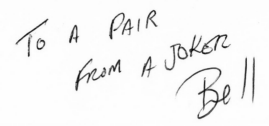

TO A PAIR
FROM A JOKER
Bell

This book is for you, dear reader.

May these ideas inspire you as you experience
the beauty and power of the words of women.

With best wishes!

marty madisall

Table of Contents

Foreword

In the stories from ancient Greece, Atalanta was renowned for her swiftness of foot as well as her ability as a hunter. When her father urged her to marry, she declared she would only marry a man who could outrun her. If the challenger failed to win, he would die. Atalanta cost many a man his life by her speed and savvy.

The symbolism of women achieving, especially at the expense of men, is a rare story. It is even less common to have myths retell the story of a woman who used brains and brawn together to succeed.

In *The Athena Treasury*, Marty Maskall has selected 101 quotations from women who have achieved in their own fields. These ideas complement her first book, *The Attitude Treasury: 101 Inspiring Quotations*. In her second book, Maskall has chosen uplifting words that may help others to achieve their goals, for it is through inspiration that our creative powers can be released.

As a professional athlete, businesswoman and fellow author, I admire women such as Atalanta, Martha Graham, Golda Meir and others in this book. I encourage each of you to combine the powers of your mind and your body, which together can create and achieve in ways that alone they cannot. But even more importantly, I urge you to balance carefully your mind and body with your spiritual self, that part deep inside which tries to live in consideration of all things. It is this synergy of mind, body, and spirit that leads to self-empowerment.

As you read the pages of *The Athena Treasury*, take time to apply the words to your own life. Allow the women who have written these words to serve as models for you, as you evolve into a model for others.

Be aware, also, of the "101st Phenomenon." This phenomenon shows that, after 100 repetitions, it is common for a new pattern to emerge. Who knows what positive changes can come from being inspired a hundred and one times?

Read on. It is only then that you, like Atalanta, can become inspired to search for life's real treasury: living fully.

Sally Edwards
Founder and President, Fleet Feet, Inc.

Preface

The *Athena Treasury* was inspired by my belief that women need models of success. As a young girl, I wanted to be a doctor. However, I saw very few female doctors, and I ended up choosing a more traditional profession. If this collection provides hope for the next generation of females and support for my sisters, then I will consider it a success. I encourage young women to read voraciously and to write passionately.

For centuries, women have been discouraged from writing and often discredited when they did write. George Sand (Aurore Dupin) and George Eliot (Mary Ann Evans) both chose to take a man's name to avoid discrimination. Even today, women's authorship is often dropped or changed to initials. As a result, quotations by women are difficult to find.

I chose Athena, the Greek goddess of wisdom and war, as the inspiration for the title because she represents a historical image of a powerful woman. The first child of Zeus, she was the most powerful of the goddesses, and her intelligence and might were widely respected. She promoted the arts and industry through her inventions which included the loom, the flute, the plow, and olive oil.

I am aware that ancient Greek society, particularly Athens, subjugated women. Nevertheless, mythology was a way of bringing the divine down to earth, and we are free to believe or doubt mythology as we please. Athena represents a tradition of wisdom, courage and strength, from which we should take the best and leave the rest.

The Author Index is a useful reference for brief information about each of the women in this collection.

The Chapter Titles reflect important qualities for a successful and happy life:

Dreams	The start of all accomplishment.
Realities	To increase understanding.
Wisdom	Helpful words to live by.
Perspective	To keep in balance.
Courage	To meet life's challenges.
Guidance	Spiritual encouragement.
Comfort	Cheerful thoughts.
Afterglow	Light that lingers in your soul.

I hope that you, the reader, will experience the beauty and power of the words of women and that these words will make a positive difference in your life.

Marty Maskall
Fair Oaks, California
March 1993

Artistic Notes

From the Cover Designers:

"Showing two faces of strength as goddess of wisdom and war, Athena is sometimes pictured with her favorite bird, the owl. Often she carries a spear and shield. As this book celebrates the wise sayings of women, we centered on the owl, now popularly recognized as a symbol of wisdom, and we eliminated the weapons. This particular owl is our version of one found on an Athenian coin circa 440 BC. The cover design, with Athena's image in flat profile, models the style of illustration popular in ancient Greece. We stayed with the earth tones used widely during that time. We felt challenged and excited to use computer technology to blend the ancient and the modern."

Gaelyn and Bram Larrick

Gaelyn and Bram Larrick, Lightbourne Images, are a computer graphics design and illustration team who specialize in book and album covers. They live and work near Clear Lake in northern California.

From the Illustrator:

"Creating these illustrations has been a labor of love, for I have long admired the vigor and inventiveness of Greek art, and my travels in Greece have only intensified my respect. In these collage-drawings, I have frequently returned to authentic images from ancient Greek sources,* blending the time-tested images with my own to honor the work of women writers.

Greek art offers timeless testaments to female beauty. The women of the magnificent vases, frescoes, and sculptures reflect both grace and strength. Consider Athena as she appears in the *Courage* chapter artwork. Athena, with her flowing robes and serene countenance, also is comfortable with the shield and spear of battle. She offers a vision of woman as both sensitive and strong."

Diane Carlson

Diane Carlson, artist and poet, lives and works in Fair Oaks, California. Her artwork and poetry are rich in nature images. Diane, who has a BA from UC Berkeley and an MA from California State University at Sacramento, teaches art in her studio. She also teaches English for Sierra College and Consumnes River College.

*The following Dover Publications (N.Y.) books were helpful with this project: *Symbols, Signs and Signets* by Ernst Lehner, and *Decorative Symbols and Motifs for Artists and Craftspeople* by Flinders Petrie.

Dreams

The Future Belongs

The future belongs
   to those who believe
   in the beauty of their dreams.

Eleanor Roosevelt

Believe in Yourself

Believe that you have the destiny, the innate ability, to become all you expect of life. Experience all of life's peaks and plateaus. Find the meaning of life's struggles and accomplishments. There you will find the meaning of life and life's work.

Trust in your deeply hidden feelings, because they show the person that you are. Take hold of each opportunity, and make the most of it.

Know the person that you are, the needs that your life contains. Search deeply to capture the essence of life. Find your limitations and build upon them. Create within yourself a person who is strong and capable of withstanding pain.

Know that life will offer some disappointments, but remember, through those situations you become a stronger, more stable person. Don't overlook obstacles, but work through them. Remember that each road you choose will offer some difficulty.

If life were meant to be easy, there would be no challenges and no rainbows.

Sherrie Householder

Life Is a Corridor of Doors

Life is a corridor of doors waiting for us
    to open them...
Life's crises are best survived by those
    who celebrate each day,
    who are fired by their goals, and
    who are renewed by their loves.

Arabella Bengson

Follow Your Dreams

Whatever you do, believe in yourself.

Follow your dreams.
　　You're going to hurt,
　　and you're going to cry.
But don't give up.

It's so rewarding
　　once you get through the struggle.
And believe me,
　　you will get through the struggle.

　　　　　　　　　　　　Amelia McCoy

All You Need to Know

Don't concern yourself with
　　how you're going to achieve your goals.
Leave that to a power greater than yourself.
All you need to know
　　is where you are going
　　　　and the answers will come to you.

　　　　　　　　　　　　Dorothea Brandt

All Things Are Possible

All things are possible
until they are proved impossible—
and even the impossible
    may only be so as of now.

Pearl S. Buck

Credo

This became a credo of mine...
    Attempt the impossible
        in order to improve your work.

Bette Davis

A Strange New Thing

At first people refuse to believe
    that a strange new thing can be done,
and then they begin to hope
    it can be done,
then they see it can be done—

then it is done,
and all the world wonders
    why it was not done centuries ago.

Frances Hodgson Burnett

Hopes and Dreams

"Hope" is the thing with feathers
  That perches in the soul...
And sings the tune without words
  And never stops...at all.

Emily Dickinson

Wonder

If children are to keep alive
    the inborn sense of wonder
    without any such gift from the fairies,
they need the companionship
    of at least one adult who can share it,
    rediscovering the joy, excitement,
    and mystery of the world we live in.

Rachel Carson

Dreams Are Possibilities

Dreams are possibilities waiting to come true.

The courage it takes
    to allow these dreams to be shared
    is minimal
    compared to the strength it ensures.

So many people
    are encompassed by outside forces
    they forget to allow themselves
    to have this courage,
but once it is found and revealed
    the rewards are limitless.

Carla Jolyn Carey

Dream and Reality

To find the point
    where hypothesis and fact meet;
the delicate equilibrium
    between dream and reality;
the place where fantasy and earthly things
    are metamorphosed into a work of art;
the hour when faith in the future
    becomes knowledge of the past;

to lay down one's power for others in need;
to shake off the old ordeal
    and get ready for the new;
to question, knowing that never
    can the full answer be found;
to accept uncertainties quietly,
    even our incomplete knowledge of God:

this is what our journey is about, I think.

Lillian Smith

Realities

What Is Reality?

I refuse to be intimidated by reality anymore.
After all, what is reality anyway?
    Nothin' but a collective hunch...
I made some studies, and
    reality is the leading cause of stress
    amongst those in touch with it.
I can take it in small doses,
    but as a lifestyle I found it too confining.

Jane Wagner

Self-Confidence

Self-confidence is so relaxing. There is no strain or stress when one is self-confident. Our lack of self-confidence comes from trying to be someone we aren't. No wonder we do not feel confident when we are living a lie.

When we realize that the best we have to bring to any situation is being just who we are, we relax. People who are cocky often show an alarming lack of self-confidence. They don't know what they have to offer.

When we know what we have to offer and we bring it to each situation, that's all we need to do.

Anne Wilson Schaef

You Can Only Decide

You don't get to choose
    how you're going to die,
    or when.
You can only decide
    how you're going to live.
    Now!

Joan Baez

Those Who Do Not Know

Those who do not know
    how to weep
        with their whole heart
do not know
    how to laugh either.

Golda Meir

The Hen and the Rooster

It's the rooster
    that does all the crowing,
but it's the hen
    that delivers the goods.

Ann Richards

Models

My female model
is my mother
a traditional
non-professional
woman at home
with high standards
on how to run a house

My male models
are the men in the office
working sixty hours a week
because they have
wives like my mother
taking care of everything

If I'm like the men
I have no time for anything
except work
evening meetings
and out-of-town business

If I'm like my mother
I have no time for anything
except keeping the house spotless
having hot meals on time
and chauffering the children

The world needs new models.
We must be these models.

Natasha Josefowitz

On the Road to Success

You'll need
a helmet for the knocks
a cushion for the falls
a mop for the tears
earplugs for the gossip
two good pairs of shoes for
    running twice as fast as the
    others in order to get to the
    same place at the same time
a hammer to nail down promises
a key to open closed minds
a hatchet to open closed doors
a gavel to command attention
a microphone so you'll be heard
a box to pick up the pieces
a friend for the good times,
    and especially for the bad times

And you might as well pack
a certificate of merit
a gold staff
the Medal of Honor
the Purple Heart
a badge of courage
    AND A HALO

Natasha Josefowitz

The Top Rung of the Ladder

One only gets to the top rung on the ladder
by steadily climbing up one at a time,
    and suddenly all sorts of powers,
    all sorts of abilities which you thought
    never belonged to you—
suddenly become
    within your own possibility and you think,

    "Well, I'll have a go, too."

Margaret Thatcher

Your Life Force

There is a vitality, a life-force, an energy, a quickening that is translated through you into action. And because there is only one of you in all of time, this expression is unique. And if you block it, it will never exist through any other medium and will be lost. The world will not have it. It is not your business to determine how good it is nor how valuable nor how it compares with other expressions.

It is your business to keep it yours clearly and directly, to keep the channel open...whether you choose to take an art class, keep a journal, record your dreams, dance your story or live each day from your own creative source.

Above all else, keep the channel open!

Martha Graham

Whatever Women Do

Whatever women do they must do
    twice as well as men to be thought
    half as good.
Luckily, this is not difficult.

Charlotte Whitton

To Shake Hands

You cannot shake hands
    with a clenched fist.

Indira Gandhi

Mother Corn

Mother Corn has fed you,
   as she has fed all Hopi people,
   since long, long ago
when she was no larger than my thumb.

Mother Corn is a promise of food and life.
I grind with gratitude
   for the richness of our harvest,
not with cross feelings
   of working too hard.

As I kneel at my grinding stone,
I bow my head in prayer,
thanking the great forces for provision.

I have received much.

I am willing to give much in return...
There must be a giving back
   for what one receives.

Sevenka Qoyawayma

21

Today

Life is a series of todays
    which so quickly turn into yesterdays
    that some of us spend our time
        looking regretfully backward.
Still others,
    through worry or procrastination,
    are always waiting for tomorrow.
In either case,
    there's the real danger of overlooking
    a very important day...today.
For this is the place and the time for living.

Let us live each day abundantly and
    beautifully while it is here.

Esther Baldwin York

Wisdom

A Mature Person

A mature person is one
    who does not think only in absolutes,
who is able to be objective even
    when deeply stirred emotionally,
who has learned that there is both
    good and bad in all people
    and in all things,
and who walks humbly and deals charitably
    with the circumstances of life,
 knowing that in this world
    no one is all-knowing,
and therefore all of us need
    both love and charity.

Eleanor Roosevelt

Accept Whatever Comes

You have to accept whatever comes
and the only important thing
    is that you meet it with courage
    and with the best you have to give.

Eleanor Roosevelt

No One Can Make You Feel Inferior

Remember,
    no one can make you feel inferior
        without your consent.

Eleanor Roosevelt

Where There's a Will, There's a Way

Faith is wanting something with all your heart. Faith is taking a chance on something before you are sure how everything will work out.

Almost anything can be accomplished by the person who really wants to succeed. But no one will ever believe they can move a mountain unless they really *want* that mountain to move. Apply this definition of faith to your dreams.

To begin, you must *know* what you want. Many people fail because they neglect to visualize in detail what they are trying to achieve. If you really want your dreams to come true, you will plan, organize, reorganize and work until you get what you want. You never really fail until you stop wanting.

It's sad that many people never commit their lives to something that has the prospect of greatness because they fear failure. Many people deliberately set their goals too low to reduce the possibility of disappointment. Obviously our goals must be realistic but high enough so that success causes us to stretch.

You also must dare to risk public criticism. It's true that most projects are criticized by negative people, but you must turn deaf ears to this criticism.

I remember when Mary Kay Cosmetics was just a dream in my heart. My attorney told me I must not risk my life's savings on this project, especially since I was a grandmother and had no experience in the cosmetics business. And for added encouragement, he even showed me a pamphlet which reported how many cosmetics companies went broke every morning.

My accountant said, "You cannot give the kind of commissions you are proposing. You'll go broke." Another cosmetics company offered to buy our formulations during our second month in business. Now we outsell them by a great margin each year!

So you must *dare*. Remember, mountain-moving faith is not just dreaming and desiring. It is also daring to risk failure.

Now you must *begin,* for "beginning is half done." We all know people who think great ideas and dream daring dreams who never get started. Even if you don't have all the details worked out in your mind, start. The pieces will fall into place.

Give it all you've got. When we expect to win, we don't hold anything back. Most people fail, not because they lack ability, intelligence or opportunity. They just fail to give their all. When you expect success, you sink your last dime and spend your second wind and energy, confident you'll make it. It is this extreme dedication that can lead to success.

Mary Kay Ash

Love Is a Fruit in Season

Love is a fruit in season at all times,
and within reach of every hand.
Anyone may gather it and no limit is set.
Everyone can reach this love through
meditation, spirit of prayer and sacrifice,
by an intense inner life.

Mother Teresa

Hard Work Never Hurt Anyone

Hard work never hurt anyone—
It's lack of it that destroys people.

Katharine Hepburn

Achievement and Success

My mother drew a distinction
    between achievement and success.
She said that achievement is the knowledge
    that you have studied and worked hard
    and done the best that is in you.

Success is being praised by others,
    and that's nice, too,
but not as important or satisfying.

Always aim for achievement
    and forget about success.

Helen Hayes

One Can Never Consent to Creep

One can never consent to creep
    when one feels an impulse to soar.

Helen Keller

When One Door Closes

When one door of happiness closes,
    another opens.
But often we look so long
    at the closed door
    that we do not see the one
        which has been opened for us.

Helen Keller

Life Is a Daring Adventure

Security is mostly a superstition.
It does not exist in nature,
    nor do people as a whole experience it.
Avoiding danger is no safer in the long run
    than outright exposure.

Life is either a daring adventure, or nothing.

Helen Keller

My Chief Duty

I long to accomplish a great and noble task,
    but it is my chief duty
    to accomplish small tasks
as if they were great and noble.

Helen Keller

Love and Service

Join the great company of those who make the barren places of the earth fruitful with kindness. Carry a vision of heaven in your hearts, and you shall make your home, your school, your world correspond to that vision.

Your success and happiness lie within you. External conditions are the accidents of life, its outer trappings. The great enduring realities are love and service. Joy is the holy fire that keeps our purpose warm and our intelligence aglow.

Resolve to keep happy, and your joy and you shall form an invisible host against difficulty. Happiness cannot come from without. It must come from within. It is not what we see and touch or that which others do for us which makes us happy; it is that which we think and feel and do, first for the other person and then for ourselves.

Helen Keller

Perspective

Letting Go

When I am all hassled about something,
    I always stop and ask myself
    what difference it will make
    in the evolution of the human species
    in the next ten million years,
and that question always helps me to get back
    my perspective.

Anne Wilson Schaef

Obstacles

Obstacles often are not personal attacks;
    they are muscle builders.

Anne Wilson Schaef

If I Had My Life to Live Over

If I had my life to live over,
  I'd dare to make more mistakes next time.
I'd relax, I would limber up.
I would be sillier than I have been this trip.
I would take fewer things seriously.
I would take more chances.
I would climb more mountains
  and swim more rivers.
I would eat more ice cream and less beans.
I would perhaps have more actual troubles,
  but I'd have fewer imaginary ones.

You see, I'm one of those people
  who lives sensibly and sanely
  hour after hour, day after day.
Oh, I've had my moments,
  and if I had it to do over again,
  I'd have more of them.
In fact, I'd try to have nothing else.
Just moments, one after another,
  instead of living so many years
  ahead of each day.
I've been one of those persons who never
  goes anywhere without a thermometer,
  a hot water bottle, a raincoat and a parachute.
If I had to do it again,
  I would travel lighter than I have.

If I had my life to live over,
  I would start barefoot earlier in the spring
  and stay that way later in the fall.
I would go to more dances.
I would ride more merry-go-rounds.
I would pick more daisies.

Nadine Stair

We All Live with the Objective

We all live
    with the objective
        of being happy;
Our lives are all different
    and yet the same.

Anne Frank

Work Gives Satisfaction

Laziness may appear attractive,
    but
Work gives satisfaction.

Anne Frank

Keep Us, O God, from Pettiness

Keep us, O God, from pettiness;
    let us be large in thought,
    in word, in deed.
Let us be done with fault-finding
    and leave off self-seeking.

May we put away all pretense
    and meet each other face-to-face—
    without self-pity and without prejudice.
May we never be hasty in judgment
    and always generous.

Let us take time for all things;
    make us to grow calm, serene, gentle.
Teach us to put into action our better
impulses, straightforward and unafraid.

Grant that we may realize it is the
    little things that create differences,
    that in the big things of life we are at one.

And may we strive to touch
    and to know the great,
    common human heart of us all, and,
    O Lord God, let us forget not to be kind!

Mary Stewart

Love the Moment

Love the moment,
    and the energy of that moment
        will spread
beyond all boundaries.

Corita Kent

Success

Life is a succession of moments.
    To live each one is to succeed.

Corita Kent

Our Happiness Depends

The greater part of our happiness or misery
    depends on our disposition
        and not on our circumstances.

Martha Washington

Winning May Not Be Everything

Winning may not be everything,
but losing has little to recommend it.

Dianne Feinstein

Don't Compromise Yourself

Don't compromise yourself.
  You are all you've got.

Janis Joplin

Warning

When I am an old woman I shall wear purple
    with a red hat which doesn't go,
    and doesn't suit me.
And I shall spend my pension
    on brandy and summer gloves
    and satin sandals,
    and say we've no money for butter.
I shall sit down on the pavement when I'm tired
    and gobble up samples in shops
    and press alarm bells
    and run my stick along the public railings
    and make up for the sobriety of my youth.
I shall go out in my slippers in the rain and
    pick the flowers in other people's gardens
    and learn to spit.

You can wear terrible shirts and grow more fat
    and eat three pounds of sausages at a go
    or only bread and pickles for a week.
And hoard pens and pencils
    and beermats and things in boxes.

But now we must have clothes that keep us dry
    and pay our rent and not swear in the street
    and set a good example for the children.
We must have friends to dinner
    and read the papers.

But maybe I ought to practice a little now?
So people who know me are not too shocked
    and surprised when suddenly I am old,
    and start to wear purple.

Jenny Joseph

Courage Is the Price

Courage is the price
     that life exacts
for granting peace.

Amelia Earhart

Courage

Courage Is Not the Absence of Fear

I want my children to know that their mother
was not a victim. She was a messenger.

I do not want them to think, as I once did,
    that courage is the absence of fear.
Courage is the strength to act wisely
    when we are most afraid.

I want them to have the courage to step
forward when called by their nation,
or their party, and give leadership—
    no matter what the personal cost.
I ask no more of you
    than I ask of myself,
        or of my children.

Mary Fisher

Go with the Pain

Go with the pain, let it take you...

Open your palms and your body to the pain.
It comes in waves like a tide, and you must
be open as a vessel lying on the beach,
letting it fill you up and then, retreating,
leaving you empty and clear...

With a deep breath—
    it has to be as deep as the pain—
one reaches a kind of inner freedom from
pain, as though the pain were not yours
but your body's.

The spirit lays the body on the altar.

Anne Morrow Lindbergh

The Challenges of Change

The challenges of change are always hard.
It is important that we begin to unpack those
challenges that confront this nation and
realize that we each have a role that requires
us to change and become more responsible for
shaping our own future.

Hillary Rodham Clinton

We Are Not Interested

We are not interested in
     the possibilities of defeat.

Queen Victoria

When You Get into a Tight Place

When you get into a tight place
     and everything goes against you
     'til it seems as though
     you could not hang on a minute longer,
never give up then,
     for that is just the place and time
     that the tide will turn.

Harriet Beecher Stowe

Nothing in Life Is to Be Feared

Nothing in life is to be feared.
It is only to be understood.

Marie Curie

Dare to Be Powerful

When I dare to be powerful—
    to use my strength
    in the service of my vision,
then it becomes less and less important
    whether I am afraid.

Audre Lorde

Never Doubt

Never doubt
    that a small group
    of thoughtful, committed citizens
    can change the world.
Indeed, it's the only thing that ever has.

Margaret Mead

Can-do Attitude

This country wasn't built on cynicism.
It was built on a can-do attitude.

One shouldn't complain about
    the way things are
unless one is willing to try
    to make a difference.

Frankie Sue del Papa

Risk

Risk! Risk anything!
Care no more for the opinion of others,
    for those voices.
Do the hardest thing on earth for you.
    Act for yourself.
        Face the truth.

Katherine Mansfield

I Have Met Brave Women

I have met brave women who are exploring
the outer edge of human possibility,
with no history to guide them, and
with a courage to make themselves vulnerable
that I find moving beyond words.

Gloria Steinem

The Dark Night of the Soul

When you go through
    the dark night of the soul,
you let go of all the old securities
    that structured your faith
    or gave shape to hope.
You surrender to the assumption
    that what brought us into being
    is far bigger
than we can ever comprehend.

Joanna Macy

Your Mission

If you cannot on the ocean
    Sail among the swiftest fleet,
Rocking on the highest billows,
    Laughing at the storms you meet,
You can stand among the sailors,
    Anchored yet within the bay.
You can lend a hand to help them,
    As they launch their boats away.

If you are too weak to journey
    Up the mountain, steep, and high,
You can stand within the valley
    While the multitude go by.
You can chant in happy measure
    As they slowly pass along.
Though they may forget the singer,
    They will not forget the song...

If you cannot in the conflict
    Prove yourself a soldier true,
If where the fire and smoke are the thickest
    There's no work for you to do,
When the battlefield is silent,
    You can go with a careful tread.
You can bear away the wounded,
    You can cover up the dead.

Do not then stand idly waiting
    For some greater work to do;
Fortune is a lazy goddess,
    She will never come to you.
Go and toil in any vineyard,
    Do not fear to do or dare.
If you want a field of labor,
    You can find it anywhere.

Ellen Gates

How to Be Really Alive

Live juicy. Stamp out conformity.
Stay in bed all day. Dream of gypsy
wagons. Find snails making love.
Develop an astounding appetite for books.
Drink sunsets. Draw out your feelings.
Amaze yourself. Be ridiculous. Stop
worrying now. If not now, then when?
Make yes your favorite word. Marry
yourself. Dry your clothes in the sun.
Eat mangoes naked. Keep toys in the
bathtub. Spin yourself dizzy. Hang
upside down. Follow a child. Celebrate
an old person. Send a love letter to yourself. Be advanced. Try endearing. Invent
new ways to love. Transform negatives.
Delight someone. Wear pajamas to a
drive-in movie. Allow yourself to feel
rich without money. Be who you truly
are and the money will follow. Believe
in everything. You are always on
your way to a miracle.

The Miracle Is You.

SARK

Guidance

The Most Useful Bit of Advice

If I were asked to give what I consider
    the single most useful bit of advice
    for all humanity,
    it would be this:

Expect trouble as an inevitable part of life
    and when it comes,
    hold your head high,
    look it squarely in the eye and say,
    "I will be bigger than you.
    You cannot defeat me."

Ann Landers

Opportunities Are Usually Disguised

Opportunities
    are usually disguised
        by hard work,
    so most people
        don't recognize them.

Ann Landers

The Best Career Advice

The best career advice to give to the young is:
    find out what you like doing best,
    and then get someone
    to pay you for doing it.

Katherine Whitehorn

Never Look Back

Make it a rule of life never to regret
    and never look back.
Regret is an appalling waste of energy;
    you can't build on it;
    it is good only for wallowing in.

Katherine Mansfield

Broken Dreams

As children brought their broken toys
    with tears for me to mend,
I brought my broken dreams to God
    because He was my friend.
But then, instead of leaving Him
    in peace to work alone,
I hung around and tried to help
    with thoughts that were my own.
Soon I snatched them back and sobbed
    "Why are You so slow?"
"My precious child," He gently sighed
    "What could I do?
        You never did let go."

Margaret Fishback Powers

Out in the Fields

The little cares that fretted me,
I lost them yesterday
    Among the fields above the sea,
    Among the winds at play;
    Among the lowing of the herds,
    The rustling of the trees,
    Among the singing of the birds,
The humming of the bees...

The foolish fears of what may happen—
I cast them all away
    Among the clover-scented grass,
    Among the new-mown hay,
    Among the hushing of the corn
    Where drowsy poppies nod,
    Where ill thoughts die and good are born
Out in the fields with God.

Elizabeth Barrett Browning

Worrying

I think these difficult times have helped me to understand better than before how infinitely rich and beautiful life is in every way, and that so many things that one goes around worrying about are or no importance whatsoever.

Isak Dinesen

A Prayer

Lord, Thou knowest better than I know myself that I am growing older, and will some day be old.

Keep me from getting talkative, and particularly from the fatal habit of thinking that I must say something on every subject and on every occasion.

Release me from craving to try to straighten out everybody's affairs.

Keep my mind free from the recital of endless details. Give me wings to get to the point.

I ask for grace enough to listen to the tales of others' pains. Help me to endure them with patience. But seal my lips on my own aches and pains. They are increasing, and my love of rehearsing them is becoming sweeter as the years go by.

Teach me the glorious lesson that occasionally it is possible that I may be mistaken.

Keep me reasonably sweet: I do not want to be a saint...some of them are so hard to live with...but a sour old person is one of the crowning works of the devil.

Make me thoughtful but not moody; helpful but not bossy. With my vast store of wisdom, it seems a pity not to use it all, but Thou knowest, Lord, that I want a few friends at the end.

Anonymous Mother Superior

Laugh and the World Laughs

Laugh and the world laughs with you,
    Weep and you weep alone;
For the sad old earth must borrow its mirth,
    But has trouble enough of its own.

Ella Wheeler Wilcox

The One Worthwhile

'Tis easy enough to be pleasant,
    When life flows along like a song;
But the one worthwhile is the one
                who will smile
    When everything goes dead wrong.

Ella Wheeler Wilcox

A Morning Prayer

Let me today do something that will take
    A little sadness from the world's vast store;
And may I be so favored as to make
    Of joy's too scanty sum a little more.

Let me not hurt, by any selfish deed
    Or thoughtless word,
                the heart of foe or friend;
Nor would I pass, unseeing, worthy need,
    Or sin by silence when I should defend.

However meager be my worldly wealth,
    Let me give something
                that shall aid my kind—
A word of courage, or a thought of health
    Dropped as I pass
                for troubled hearts to find.

Let me tonight look back across the span
    'Twixt dawn and dark,
                and to my conscience say—
Because of some good act
                to beast or human—
    "The world is better that I lived today."

Ella Wheeler Wilcox

Dear Lord I Ask

Dear Lord, I do not ask that life
May always easy be,
But that I always may have strength
For all that comes to me.

I do not ask for worldly wealth,
But this my earnest plea,
That I may know how best to use
What has been given me.

I do not ask to make new friends
But humbly, Lord, I bow,
And ask that I may faithful be
To those that I have now.

I do not ask that I may live
Where rough winds never blow,
I only ask that in my heart
Thy peace and love may glow.

Mae E. Margrat

Comfort

Oh the Comfort

Oh the comfort,
    the inexplicable comfort
        of feeling safe with a person.
Having neither to weigh thoughts
    nor measure words
    but to pour them all out just as they are,
chaff and grain together.
Knowing that a faithful hand
    will take and sift them,
    keep what is worth keeping, and then,
     with a breath of kindness,
       blow the rest away.

George Eliot

To Love and to Help

After the verb
    "To Love,"
        "To Help"
is the most beautiful verb in the world.

Bertha von Suttner

The Telephone of My Mind

I keep
    the telephone of my mind
        open to
peace, harmony, health, love, and abundance.

Then whenever
    doubt, anxiety, or fear try to call me,
        they keep getting a busy signal,
and soon they'll forget my number.

Edith Armstrong

A Full Life Depends

People need people and friends need friends,
    And we all need love
        for a full life depends
    Not on vast riches or great acclaim,
    Not on success or on worldly fame,
    But just knowing that someone cares
    And holds us close in their
        thoughts and prayers—

For only the knowledge
    that we're understood
Makes everyday living feel wonderfully good,
And we rob ourselves of life's greatest need
When we "lock up our hearts"
    and fail to heed
The outstretched hand reaching to find
A kindred spirit whose heart and mind
Are lonely and longing to somehow share
Our joys and sorrows and to make us aware
That life's completeness and richness depends
On the things we share with
    our loved ones and friends.

Helen Steiner Rice

The Ability to Present Yourself

The ability to present yourself
　　　and your ideas well
　　is to your skills and your personality
as sunshine is to a stained-glass window...

How you choose to express your ideas
is a reflection of the quality of your thinking,
and nothing contributes more to presence
than the ability to talk about
　　worthwhile things and events
　　in a worthwhile way.

Dorothy Sarnoff

Support Group

You can fall here.
We are a quilt set to catch you
A quilt of women's hands
Threaded by pain made useful.

With generations of comfort-making
Behind us, we offer this gift
Warm as grandma's featherbed
Sweet as the Heavenly Mother's
    Lullaby Song.

You can fall here.
Women's hands are strong.

Carol Lynn Pearson

You Are Not Alone

You are not alone,
though loneliness seems to follow
and consume you too often.

You are not alone.
Inside your head, three inches behind your eyes,
lie the untouched wonders of yourself.
Look there for comfort and companionship
which you seek from others in the world.

Take a minute of solitude
to empty yourself of resentment and anger
from the pressures of this hurried life.
There are other levels within you:
some to regain...which you have lost;
others to attain...if you give yourself the chance.
You have been caught in the trap of living,
rushing after love or even a sign from another
which will make you feel you are worthwhile.

Stop...reach down inside yourself.
Bring forth the other voices,
                    other faces which are yours.
Touch your own soul first, that you may better
give to others that which you seek:
love...self-worth...freedom from loneliness.
You have the power to do these things.
Find them within your own being.
Share them with compassion and tranquillity.
They will return...full circle...for you to use.
From this day forward, you are not alone.

Diane Westlake

How Can We Communicate Love?

How can we communicate love?

I think three things are involved:
    We must reach out to a person,
        make contact.
    We must listen with the heart,
        be sensitive to the other's needs.
    We must respond in a language
        that the person can understand.

Many of us do all the talking.
We must learn to listen
    and to keep on listening.

Princess Pale Moon

Worthwhile Things

Nothing is worthwhile, you know,
Unless you work to make it so;
Easy gold has easy wings,
All the solid steady things
Seem to come a slower way,
Seem to grow from day to day.

Love of home and stalwart might
Are not molded overnight,
Honesty and rugged toil
Do not grow in shallow soil,
For their roots strike deep and find
Happiness and peace of mind.

Things that last from age to age,
Handed down by heritage,
Bred in every throbbing vein,
Forged by happiness and pain,
Wrought in us until they stand
For the truest in the land.

So when you have a building task
Choose the things that will not pass;
Lay foundations strong and fair,
Put the best that's in you there.
Nothing is worthwhile unless
Thus you build for happiness.

Edna Jacques

Just Around the Corner

Just around the corner
    Is supposed to be
The place where happiness
    Waits for you and me.

Just around the corner
    Is too far away;
Be happy where you are
    Every passing day.

Right here and right now, too,
    Is the time to start,
For real happiness comes
    From within your heart.

Virginia K. Oliver

The Little Things

It's the little things in life that count,
    The things of every day;
Just the simple things that we can do,
    The kind words we can say.

The little things like a friendly smile
    For those who may be sad,
The clasp of a hand or kindly deed
    To help make someone glad.

A knock on the door of lonely homes,
    Or flowers bright and gay
For someone to whom you might bring cheer
    With just a small bouquet.

Just the little greetings here and there
    On which so much depends,
The little pleasures that all can share,
    The joy of making friends.

Virginia K. Oliver

To a Friend

Let the great out-of-doors embrace you...
　　　Let it take you in its arms...
　　　　　And caress you...
　　　　　With its cool breezes...
　　　　　And its warm sunlight...
　　　Let it thrill you with its beauty...
　　　　　And soothe you with its harmony...
　　　Let it open new doors to your soul...
　　　　　And lead new pathways to your heart...
　　　Let it weave its pattern upon your life...
　　　Let it sing to you...
Then there could not be any
　　　real darkness anywhere...
For even that will have its stars.

Lorice Fiani Mulhern

Afterglow

Stars Veil Their Beauty

Stars veil their beauty soon
Beside the glorious moon,
When her full silver light
Doth make the whole earth bright.

Sappho

God's World

Oh world, I cannot hold thee close enough!
    Thy winds, thy wide grey skies!
    Thy mists, that roll and rise!
Thy woods, this autumn day,
    that ache and sag
And all but cry with colour! That gaunt crag
To crush! To lift the lean of that black bluff!
World, World, I cannot get thee close enough!

Long have I known a glory in it all,
    But never knew I this;
    Here such a passion is
As stretcheth me apart,—Lord, I do fear
Thou'st made the world
    too beautiful this year;
My soul is all but out of me,—let fall
No burning leaf; prithee, let no bird call.

Edna St. Vincent Millay

One Cheering Word

If I have said one cheering word
    or done a helpful deed,
If I have smoothed one rocky path
    or filled a special need,
If I have eased one doubt or fear
    or chased one cloud away,
If I have brought one person joy...
    then I've lived well today.

Amanda Bradley

Life's Pattern

Life's threads all form a pattern,
   Some silver. Some of gold.
And there are new and finer threads
   to mingle with the old.
Some tiny threads are broken,
   a stitch or two is skipped,
But when the work is finished,
   the pattern isn't ripped.
It forms a perfect blending
   of all of life's great dreams.
With love we frame the border—
   with sorrow sew the seams.
So fold the pattern to your heart.
   Sweet memories are the dearest part.

Charlotte Trevillyan Sheward

Today I Smiled

Today I smiled, and all at once
    Things didn't look so bad.
Today I shared with someone else,
    A bit of hope I had.
Today I sang a little song,
    And felt my heart grow light,
And walked a happy little mile,
    With not a cloud in sight.

Today I worked with what I had,
    Nor longed for any more,
And what had seemed like only weeds,
    Were flowers at my door.
Today I loved a little more,
    Complained a little less,
And in the giving of myself,
    Forgot my weariness.

Grace Easley

Just Do Your Best

Just do your best
In whatever you do,
Though sometimes it may not
Be easy for you.
Half-heartedness never
Accomplished a goal,
And positive thinking
Is food for the soul.

Just do your best,
That's all one can ask,
In spite of the odds,
Whatever the task.

So what if you work up
Some old fashioned sweat?
You first have to give
Before you can get.

Just do your best
With what you have got,
And though it is little,
Or if it's a lot,
You'll know in your heart,
When each day is through,
You've done everything
God expected of you.

Grace Easley

But Not Today

I shall grow old, perhaps, but not today,
Not while my hopes are young,
                    my spirit strong,
My vision clear, because life has a way
Of smoothing out the wrinkles with a song.

I shall grow old, perhaps, but not today,
Not while my dreams remain
                    a shining shield,
My faith a lance, and 'neath a sky of grey,
My colors wave upon the battlefield.

I shall grow old, perhaps, but not today,
Not while this pen can write upon a page,
And memories turn Winter into May,
Shall this stout heart be brought to terms
                    by age.

I shall grow old, perhaps, but not today,
And scorning Time, who would enlist
                    my tears,
I stand convinced there is a better way,
Of occupying all the coming years.

I shall grow old, perhaps, but not today,
In my own style and in my own sweet time,
No night so dark there does not fall a ray
Of light along the pathway that I climb.

Just say of me, when my last hour slips
Like one bright leaf to softly rest among
The others..."Life was Summer to the heart,
Of one who died believing she was young."

Grace Easley

A Lovely Light

A candle is but a simple thing,
It starts with just a bit of string,
Yet dipped and dipped, with patient hand,
It gathers wax upon the strand
Until complete and snowy white,
It gives at last a lovely light.

Life seems so like that bit of string!
Each deed we do, a simple thing...
Yet day by day if on life's strand
We work with patient heart and hand,
It gathers joy, makes dark days bright,
And gives at last a lovely light.

Clara Bell Thurston

Tomorrow

Tomorrow does not stand apart,
   A shining, all new day;
Tomorrow is a thing slow-built
   Of hours passed away.

It's made of dreams your heart has stored,
   And dreams discarded, too;
It's made of all the joys and tears
   The years have brought to you.

It's made of lessons you have learned,
   The friend you've known—the foes;
As each of our Todays is bent,
   So our Tomorrow grows.

It's made of sweat and toil and pain
   And song and love and laughter;
Each minute of Today helps build
   The day that follows after.

Tomorrow does not spring full-built
   With some new dawn's bright rays—
Tomorrow is a slow-built thing
   Made up of Yesterdays.

Helen Lowrie Marshall

The Ingredients of Happiness

One is happy as a result of one's own efforts,
    once one knows the necessary
    ingredients of happiness—
        simple tastes,
        a certain degree of courage,
        self-denial to a point,
        love of work, and above all,
        a clear conscience.
Happiness is no vague dream,
    of that I now feel certain.

George Sand

You Never Know

You never know when someone
May catch a dream from you.
You never know when a little word
Or something you may do
May open up the windows
Of a mind that seeks the light.
The way you live may not matter at all,
But you never know—it might.

And just in case it could be
That another's life, through you,
Might possibly change for the better
With a broader and brighter view,
It seems it might be worth a try
At pointing the way to the right.
Of course, it may not matter at all,
But then again—it might.

Helen Lowrie Marshall

Love Is the Only Thing

Love is the only thing that
we can carry with us when we go,
and it makes the end so easy.

Louisa May Alcott

Afterglow

I'd like the memory of me
    to be a happy one.
I'd like to leave an afterglow
    of smiles when life is done.

I'd like to leave an echo
    whispering softly down the ways,
Of happy times and laughing times
    and bright and sunny days.

I'd like the tears of those who grieve,
    to dry before the sun
Of happy memories that I leave
    When life is done.

Helen Lowrie Marshall

Acknowledgments

This book was inspired by many friends who liked *The Attitude Treasury* and who asked for another book of quotations, particularly with quotations by women. Thanks to all of you who have encouraged me. You know who you are, even if you are not listed here. I am particularly grateful to the following individuals:

Wendy Slater for keeping me on track;
Tillie Maskall, my mother, for support and valuable suggestions;
Gaelyn Larrick for faith in the concept;
Diane Carlson for imaginative art;
Vineeta Chand for editorial assistance;
Barbara Pletcher for continuing encouragement;
Alexis Laris of Athena Enterprises, for inspiring the title idea;
John Tomich, Diane de Porter, Marj Stuart, Margo Fowkes, Cheewa James, Nancy Compton, Karen Hegglin, Nicole Williams, Roberta Sallustio, Sandy Sherman, Marian Ash, Vern Bluhm, Pam Griggsby-Jones and *Avis Ziegler* for supplying quotations;
Marlene Cartwright, Ruth Cleary, Ann Robinson, and Cheewa James for supplying quotes and reviewing the manuscript;
Virginia Stellmach, Sudesh Singal, Jody Hornor, Heather Taft, Dan Poynter, Rita Lingwood, Debbie Mirande, Nancy Blue, Toni Drinkwine, Misty Paul, Ingrid Hart, Katie Wlasiuk, Michael King, Mary Horne, Beth Rees, Paulette Pitner, Ron Curry, and Betty Piscitelli for reviewing the manuscript.

About the Editor

Marty Maskall has been collecting inspiring quotations for the past 30 years. She believes strongly in the benefits of positive thinking.

Marty is the daughter of an English teacher who taught her to love the beauty and power of words. She holds a B.A. in Biology from Stanford and an M.A. in Zoology from Duke. After taking a course in computer programming, she got the "bug" and spent 14 years in the computer field. In 1983, she became an executive recruiter, specializing in information processing. In 1990, she formed Attitude Works Publishing Company and published *The Attitude Treasury: 101 Inspiring Quotations.*

In her spare time, Marty enjoys hiking, ballroom dancing, and Toastmasters International. She is also a member of Data Processing Management Association, National Association for Professional Saleswomen, Business and Professional Women, National Organization for Women, and the Sierra Club. She organized the Towe Ford Museum Speakers Bureau. She has a Distinguished Toastmaster designation and a Certificate in Data Processing, and she is listed in *Who's Who of American Women* and *Who's Who in the West.*

Title Index

Author Index

Includes Titles, Brief Biographical Information

Bibliography

Grateful acknowledgment is given to the original authors of these works. Diligent attempts have been made to trace the source of the passages and to give proper credit. If there are errors, they will gladly be corrected in the next edition if written notification is received by the publisher.

A few passages have been adapted to eliminate male-centered language and to make their appeal more general. These passages are noted by the word "adapted" in the list below. For rewording, I have used guidelines suggested by Casey Miller and Kate Swift in their *Handbook of Nonsexist Writing*, (New York, NY: Harper & Row, 1988).

References are listed below:

Ash, Mary Kay. Where There's a Will, There's a Way, from *From My Heart*. Mary Kay Cosmetics. Dallas, TX. 1992. Reprinted with permission.

Bengson, Arabella. Life is a Corridor of Doors, from "Midlife: Crisis or Opportunity." Speech to Toastmasters International convention, Washington, D.C., 1988. Reprinted with permission of the author.

Carey, Carla Jolyn. Dreams Are Possibilities. Reprinted with permission of the author.

Carson, Rachel. Wonder. Adapted.

Del Papa, Frankie Sue. Can-do Attitude. Speech 6/19/92 at Toastmasters Regional Convention, Reno, NV. Reprinted with permission.

Fisher, Mary. Courage Is Not the Absence of Fear. Speech to the Republican National Convention, August 10, 1992. Reprinted with permission.

Fishback, Margaret Powers. Broken Dreams. *Heart to Heart Collection.* 1972. Reprinted with permission of the author.

Hepburn, Katharine. Hard Work Never Hurt Anyone. Quoted in television interview, *All About Me,* January 18, 1993.

Joseph, Jenny. Warning, from *Rose in the Afternoon.* J. M. Dent and Sons. England.

Josefowitz, Natasha.
Models, from *Natasha's Words for Friends,* Warner, 1986.
On the Road to Success, from *Paths to Power: A Woman's Guide from First Job to Top Executive.* Reprinted with permission.

Keller, Helen. Life Is a Daring Adventure, from *The Open Door,* Doubleday. Adapted.

Macy, Joanna. The Dark Night of the Soul. Reprinted with permisison of the author.

Mansfield, Katherine, Risk. Journals.

Margrat, Mae. Dear Lord I Ask, from *Pages from My Old Book of Memories.*

McCoy, Amelia. Follow Your Dreams. Founder, Handmade Rainbows and Halos by Amelia Inc. In NASE Newspaper, Self-Employed America, July 1992.

Mother Superior, Anonymous. A Prayer. Appeared in *Ideals* V27 #1, January 1970.

Mulhern, Lorice. To a Friend, from *Realms of Enchantment,* Dorrance & Co. 1970.

Oliver, Virginia K. Just Around the Corner and The Little Things. Reprinted with permission of her executor.

Pearson, Carol Lynn. Support Group, from *Women I Have Known & Been,* Aspen Books, Salt Lake City, UT. Reprinted with permission of the author.

Princess Pale Moon. How Can We Communicate Love?, from *Pale Moon: Stories of an Indian Princess*. American Indian Heritage Foundation. Washington, D.C. 1974. Used by permission of the author.

Richards, Ann. Quoted by Senator Dianne Feinstein in her 1992 Senatorial acceptance speech.

Roosevelt, Eleanor. A Mature Person, from *It Seems to Me*, 1954

SARK. How To Be Really Alive, from *A Creative Companion: How to Free Your Creative Spirit*. Celestial Arts, Berkeley CA. 1991. Reprinted with permission of the author.

Sarnoff, Dorothy. The Ability to Present Yourself, from *Make the Most of Your Best*. Holt, Rinehart, Winston. NY. 1981.

Schaef, Anne Wilson. Letting Go, Obstacles, and Self-Confidence, from *Meditations for Women Who Do Too Much*, Harper Collins. 1990

Smith, Lillian. Dream and Reality, from *The Journey*, 1954. Adapted.

Stair, Nadine, age 85, Louisville, Kentucky. Published in *Family Circle*, March 27, 1978, p. 99

Steinem, Gloria. I Have Met Brave Women. Reprinted with permission of the author

Stewart, Mary. Keep Us, Oh God, from Pettiness. Written in 1904. Adopted by Business and Professional Woman as the official prayer in 1920.

Westlake, Diane. You Are Not Alone, from *Gentle Freedom*. Honor Press. Manhattan Beach, CA. Reprinted with permission of the author.

Wilcox, Ella Wheeler
A Morning Prayer. Adapted.
Laugh and the World Laughs, from *Solitude*.
The One Worthwhile. from *Worth While*. Adapted.

Many of the quotations were found in other publications, and no source was indicated or could be found. I am grateful for the use of the books listed below, and I recommend them to the reader:

Anderson, Peggy. *Great Quotes from Great Women.* Celebrating Excellence Publishing. Lombard, IL. 1992.

Campbell, Eileen. *A Dancing Star. Inspirations to guide and heal.* The Aquarian Press. London. 1991.

James, Cheewa. *Catch the Whisper of the Wind.* A book of Native American insights. Horizon 2000. Sacramento, CA. 1992.

Maggio, Rosalie. *The Beacon Book of Quotations by Women.* Beacon Press. Boston, MA. 1992.

The Quotable Woman. Running Press. Philadelphia, PA. 1991.

Schaef, Anne Wilson. *Meditations for Women Who Do Too Much.* Harper Collins. New York, NY. 1990.

Warner, Carolyn. *The Last Word. A Treasury of Women's Quotes.* Prentice Hall. Englewood Cliffs, NJ. 1992.

Other Books by Marty Maskall

The Attitude Treasury: 101 Inspiring Quotations is a much-loved collection of wisdom from the ages. Attractively arranged and thoroughly indexed for easy reference, the book makes a wonderful gift for someone special—or for yourself.

What Others Say:

Your book is great!   Og Mandino, Author
                                Greatest Salesman in the World

These beautiful quotations offer answers for any concern. I recommend a copy on every nightstand.
                                          Jane Nelson, Ed.D.
                          Author, Counselor and Speaker

An exceptional book...I shall use it often.
                                  John Fauvel, President
                      Toastmasters International, 1988

In *The Attitude Treasury* you will find 101 inspiring, comforting, and encouraging thoughts which will make a positive difference in your life.

To Order

For additional copies of *The Athena Treasury* or *The Attitude Treasury*, please send your name, address, daytime phone number, and a check payable to:

The Attitude Works Publishing Company
P. O. Box 1765B
Fair Oaks, CA 95628
(916) 967-2470

1 - 4 books	$9.95 each
5 - 9	$8.95
10 +	$7.95

Sales tax:
Please add applicable sales tax for books shipped to California addresses.

Shipping:
$2 for shipping via U.S. mail, or
$4 for United Parcel Service,
plus 50 cents for each additional book.
Allow 3 weeks for U.S. mail and 7 days for UPS.

Visa/Mastercard:
You may order by mail or phone (916/967-2470).
Please include the name on the card and the expiration date.

Fund-raising:
The Athena Treasury and *The Attitude Treasury* are available to groups for fund-raising. Please call 916/967-2470 for details.

Your satisfaction guaranteed or your money promptly refunded.